ポルトガルの植民地形成と
日本人奴隷

PORTUGUESE COLONIALISM AND JAPANESE SLAVES

Michio Kitahara

北原 惇

花伝社
Kadensha Tokyo

ポルトガルの植民地形成と
日本人奴隷

これは『なぜ太平洋戦争になったのか』(北原惇著、2001年、ＴＢＳブリタニカ発行)の第一章、「ポルトガル人による日本人奴隷売買」に筆者自身が資料を追加し、より詳細に書き直したものである。

目　　次

まえがき　7

序論　11
海外の日本人奴隷　11
日本人が奴隷になった理由　14
秀吉の激怒　15
ポルトガル側の態度と反応　18
奴隷売買禁止の効果　20
奴隷売買の禁止が失敗した理由　23
日本側の行動　25
これらの出来事の解釈　27
結論　29

注ならびに文献　31

まえがき

　殺人事件があったとする。そして犯人と見なされる人間が逮捕され、裁判になり、審議の結果、裁判長が「被告は殺したかったので殺した」という判断を示し、終身刑の判決になったとする。
　いくら刑法のいいかげんな国でも、このような裁判をし判決を下す例は世界でもあまりないのではなかろうか。殺人事件の裁判ともなれば、検察側も弁護側も手に入るあらゆる資料に目を通し、殺人にいたるまでのいきさつ、被告の心理状態と人間関係、殺人になった時点での社会環境などあらゆる要素を考察して事件への対応をするのが文明国の常識である。すべての事件にはそれに先行する重大な出来事があったものと仮定し、それらの出来事すべてを慎重に考察した上で客観的な判決にいたるのが法治国である。しかし驚くべきことには、歴史の解釈には「殺したかったので殺した」式の説明が多い。
　その一例は真珠湾の攻撃である。欧米でかなり一般的に理解されている真珠湾攻撃という事件の説明は次のようなものである。「日本では1920年代から国粋主義、軍国主義、侵略主義が台頭し、ナチスのドイツ、ファッシズムのイタリアと連携し、真珠湾を攻撃し、第二次世界大戦にアメリカを参戦させた」。これは国の違いに関係なく、マス・メディア、初等・中等教育の教科書などでごく一般的に観察される説明である。
　ここで問題なのは真珠湾攻撃は国粋主義、軍国主義、侵略主義などを集約した具体的行動であるという事実である。歴史上の具体的な出来事をより一般的な歴史的事実によって説明して理解しているつもりであるが、これでは説明にならない。真珠湾攻撃という特殊な出来事を理解するには国粋主義、軍国主義、侵略主義がなぜ日本で形成され、それがな

ぜ真珠湾攻撃にいたったのかを説明しなければならない。国粋主義、軍国主義、侵略主義は日本である日突然発生したものではなく、それに先行した数々の事件によって理解され説明されなければならない。しかしこれは欧米の常識では欠如している。このような「殺したかったから殺した」式の歴史観が世界の「常識」である。

欧米の大学や学会などでは「日本は人口密度が高く資源が不足していたため」、「日本人は人種的優越感のために中国を侵略し、それを欧米に批判されたため」、などという説明がかなり広く流布され、欧米にとって都合のわるい説明は無視されてしまう傾向が明確である。

戦後の日本では占領軍が日本人の徹底的な思想改革を強制し、ナチスのドイツ同様、「日本は悪者であった」という教育をした。そしてその方針に従った学説や思想が日本を支配し、それ以外の学説や思想は排除され無視された。この占領軍の方針に従った説明の場合、単に真珠湾攻撃をした日本は悪者であった、という解釈だけでなく、それ以前に日本の歴史上で起こった一連の出来事もすべて「日本は悪者であった」という解釈に従った説明にされた。

その良い例が鶴見俊輔が1956年に初めて用いたとされる「十五年戦争」という表現である。これは1931年の満州事変から1945年のポツダム宣言受諾にいたるまでの約14年間に日本が関与していた戦争すべてを一括して考慮し、これを日本の国粋主義、軍国主義、侵略主義の思想的集約と見なす考えである。この解釈によって「悪者としての日本」の文化と歴史に真珠湾攻撃を明確に説明できる根拠が存在するという議論ができるわけである。

しかしこの「十五年戦争」の説明は、真珠湾攻撃にいたる以前の日本史上の極度に重要な出来事を無視している。日本の歴史を振り返ってみると、満州事変が起こった時点以前に真珠湾攻撃を理解するのに不可欠な数多くの歴史的な事実がある。これらの事実を無視してはならない。それは日本が欧米の植民主義、侵略主義、人種主義に対決させられたた

めに起こった歴史的事実である。

　真珠湾攻撃を理解するには、それをより客観的に理解するための歴史的事実を求めて日本の歴史を再考しなければならない。それには日本の歴史をどこまでさかのぼればよいであろうか。林房雄はこの点に着目し、「東亜百年戦争」という表現を用いている。これは、太平洋戦争（林房雄は「大東亜戦争」という表現を用いている）を理解するにはポツダム宣言の受諾から約百年さかのぼった時点からの日本史を考察しなければならない、という主張である。この百年というのは日本が欧米の植民主義、侵略主義、人種主義に直面させられた百年である。これは大変重要な解釈であり、「十五年戦争」の解釈よりも正確で客観的な歴史観であり評価されなければならない。

　しかし真珠湾攻撃を理解するためにはこの百年間の歴史的事実の考察をするだけで充分であろうか。筆者はこの百年をさらに拡大し、日本史をさらにさかのぼり、種子島の時点までとしなければならないと主張する。林房雄の百年をさらに延長して四百年にするわけである。種子島以来、南蛮人の渡来、南蛮貿易、キリシタンの導入、鉄砲の普及、日本人奴隷の海外輸出、キリシタン厳禁、鎖国、といった一連の歴史的事実を理解して初めて真珠湾攻撃が理解できる、というのが筆者の主張である。

　キリシタン厳禁とオランダ人以外の欧米人追放の後、日本は二百年以上も鎖国を実行した。鎖国とは外国とは付き合わない、外国には興味がない、外国とは縁を持ちたくない、外国には関わりたくない、という政策である。その鎖国政策を二百年以上も実行した日本がどうして、そしてどのようにして侵略主義、植民主義、人種主義の思想を持つようになり、それを実行したのであろうか。

「日本は悪者であった」と信じている欧米人や日本人に次のような質問をしたい。鎖国の思想を持ち、鎖国を実行していた国がある日突然外国を侵略し、植民地を持ち、人種主義を実行し始めるであろうか。この日本の極端な変容はなぜ、そしてどのようにして起こったのであろうか。

それには誰にも理解できる、納得のゆく理由があったのではなかろうか。
　歴史家トインビーは歴史を理解する鍵として「チャレンジとレスポンス」という概念を用いている。この考え方を鎖国の日本に当てはめてみると、欧米の侵略主義、植民主義、人種主義は日本にとって「チャレンジ」であり、それに対決させられた日本の「レスポンス」が日本式の侵略主義、植民主義、人種主義であった、という解釈ができる。そしてこれがより事実に近い日本史ではないかと考えられる。
　筆者はこの問題を『なぜ太平洋戦争になったのか』と題された本の中で詳しく論じた（東京、ＴＢＳブリタニカ、2001 年）。この本の第一章は「ポルトガル人による日本人奴隷売買」と題され、その内容は章のタイトルそのままである。
　この本が出版された後、多くの読者から日本人がポルトガル人によって奴隷として海外に送られていたとは知らなかった、初めて聞いた、という感想を頂いた。そこでこの事実をさらに詳しく世界に知らせておく必要を感じ、今回ここに小論文のような形の文章を出版する次第である。
　著者の立場から読者にお願いしたいのは最初にこの小論文を読んでいただき、次に『なぜ太平洋戦争になったのか』の第二章以降を読んでいただくことである。それによって筆者の主張する日本史のより客観的な考察を理解していただけるものと信じる。さらに付け加えれば、その後の日本、特に戦後の日本人の心理と日本人の幼児化現象を理解していただくには拙著の『幼児化する日本人』（東京、リベルタ出版、2005 年）も読んでいただければと感じる。筆者が日本語で出版した本はすべて西洋文明と対決した日本を取り扱っていると言ってもよい。この点にご興味のある読者にさらに別の拙著も読んでいただければ著者として最高の幸せである。

序　論

　16世紀にヨーロッパが拡大主義と植民地形成の時代に入ることによって、日本の歴史は急変した。一般には1543年に種子島に漂着した中国船に乗っていたポルトガル人との接触が、近世における日本とヨーロッパの関係の始まりと見なされている[1]。そしてやはり通説としてこの折にポルトガル人が日本に鉄砲を導入したと言われている。いずれにしても、ちょうどこの頃日本と西洋の本格的な接触が始まったと考えてまちがいない。

　これらのポルトガル人が中国船に乗って日本に渡来した事実から推測できるように、ポルトガルが商品として日本に持ち込んだ物品のほとんどは絹や香料のような中国産のものであった。このような一見平和に見える交易とともに、まったく別の種類の商売も行われていた。それはポルトガル人が日本人奴隷を海外で売ることであった。この事実は世界ではもちろんのこと、日本でもほとんど知られておらず、学校でも言及することさえないのが戦前・戦中・戦後の日本の教育の実態である。

海外の日本人奴隷

　16世紀の後半に多くの日本人がアジア各地に居住していたことが知られている。それにもかかわらず、日本人が日本を出国したという記録はほとんど残されていない。この奇妙な事実は出国した日本人は自由の身で出国したわけではなく、奴隷として出荷されたためである[2]。これらの奴隷の出荷先は植民国としてのポルトガルの支配下にあった地域、たとえばインド、東南アジア、中国南部などで、特にマカオ、マラッカ海峡周辺、そしてインドのゴアであった[3]。

　シャム（現在のタイ国）がビルマならびにラオスと戦った1585年と

1587年の戦争ではシャムの軍隊には日本兵が参加していたことが知られている[4]。一説によれば1579年にシャムがビルマとラオスに侵略されたとき、シャム軍には500人の日本兵が加わっていた[5]。しかし別の説によればこの戦争は1585年または1587年であったとのことである[6]。

　1605年にジョン・デービス指揮下のイギリス船がマレー半島のパタで日本人の海賊と戦い、デービスも日本人海賊も死亡した[7]。1606年にはオランダ人のコーネリウス・マテレイフに率いられた11隻の船がマラッカのポルトガルの植民地を攻撃したときにはポルトガル人と共に日本人兵士が応戦し、オランダ人たちを撤退させた[8]。1610年のシャムの内戦では280人の日本人兵士たちが反乱軍に参加し、アユタヤの町を占拠し、国王に各種の要求を受け入れさせることに成功した[9]。これらの記録に残されている日本兵は、実は16世紀にこれらの地域に連れ込まれた日本人奴隷であったと推測されている[10]。

　日本人奴隷はポルトガル[11]やアルゼンチン[12]にまで売られていったと思われる記録も残されている。キリスト教は1549年にイエズス会のフランシスコ・ザビエルによって日本に伝えられたが、1582年にはすでに14万5000人もの日本人信者が存在していたとも推測されている[13]。その一部は大名で、そのうち大友宗麟、有馬晴信、大村純忠の3大名は改宗した4人の少年を使節としてローマ法王に派遣することをした。これは1582年のことでイタリア人の宣教師アレキサンドロ・バリニャーノの勧告に従ったものである[14]。この少年使節団はゴアやリスボンを経由し、ローマに到着し、法王グレゴリー13世に面会し、1590年に無事日本に帰国した。4人の日本人少年によるこの異例の出来事の記録はラテン語で出版され、日本では一般に『天正遣欧使節記』として知られている。

　それによると、ミゲルという名の少年は旅行中各地で日本人奴隷を目撃し、同胞を家畜のように奴隷として安く売った日本人に憤りを覚えたと述べている。マンショという名の別の少年の反応も同様で、あれほど多数の同胞の男女や少年少女が安い値段で売られて惨めな仕事をさせら

れているのを見て同情せざるをえなかった、と述べている[15]。

　これはヨーロッパでの事情であるが、南米にも日本人奴隷が存在していたらしい記録もある。アルゼンチンのコルドバ市には1574年に創立された州立歴史博物館がある。ここに保存されている1597年の記録文書によれば、フランシスコ・ハポンという名の日本人が3月4日に裁判所に対して告訴をしている。その内容は三点からなり、自分は奴隷ではない、奴隷ではないので売買される理由はない、従って釈放されなければならない、という申し立てである。この裁判は公証人フランシスコ・デ・ソト・マジョールによって仲介され、原告の主張は認められ、フランシスコ・ハポンは1598年に自由の身になったとされている[16]。

　しかしポルトガル人だけが奴隷の売買をし、日本人だけがその犠牲になったわけではない。歴史はこれよりはるかに複雑であった。ポルトガル人たちがアジアに進出する以前にもアジアでは自国・他国の人々を奴隷にすることをしていた。例えば1274年の文永の役では日本はモンゴル人、漢人、女真人、高麗人の混成軍によって襲撃され、壱岐が占領されて多数の日本人が殺害された。この事件は高麗側の公式記録である『高麗史』の28巻に明記されている。それによると200人の少年少女が捕虜となり高麗王と王妃に奴隷として献上されたとある[17]。

　14世紀半ばから盛んに活動をしていた倭寇は対馬、壱岐、ならびに九州の松浦地方を根拠地としていたが、倭寇は日本人だけではなく高麗人も含んでおり[18]、中国や朝鮮半島からの奴隷を売ることをしていた[19]。日本人奴隷は中国やインドシナに売られていた[20]。中国人は中国人によって外国船に売られていた[21]。ポルトガル人はすでに1520年に奴隷売買をしており奴隷は中国人であった[22]。

　16世紀の後半には朝鮮半島からの奴隷が日本に送り込まれ、日本人の奴隷と共にポルトガル人に売られていた。これらの朝鮮半島からの奴隷のほとんどは1592年と1597年に日本が侵略したときに奴隷にされたもので、中国から到着したポルトガル船によって輸送されていた[23]。

日本の兵士は朝鮮で子供を捕えていたとも言われている[24]。長崎の商人が朝鮮半島からの奴隷売買にかかわっていたと言う説もある[25]。ジャバからの奴隷は特に安くリスボンに送られていた[26]。

日本人が奴隷になった理由

　日本人が奴隷になった理由は主として四つある[27]。第一に、封建制の日本では他の領地の住民を捕え、ポルトガル人に捕虜であるといつわって売りつけていた。その理由はイエズス会は捕虜の売買は大目に見ていたためである。しかし現実には戦争の結果発生した捕虜の数は多くなかったため、このようないつわりの方法による奴隷ができあがったわけである[28]。

　第二に、当時の日本の慣習のために奴隷が発生した。例えば、男が何らかの理由により死刑にされるとその妻と子供は奴隷にならざるをえなかった。また夫と生活を共にすることを拒否した妻、父親を見捨てた息子、主人のもとを去った下僕が領主のもとに逃れ、その結果奴隷になった。男が債務の支払いができない場合にも子供や親が奴隷として売られていた[29]。

　第三に、貧困のために親が子供を奴隷として売ることもあった[30]。

　第四に、日本を出国したい日本人が自らを奴隷として売ることをした[31]。これはアメリカに移住したくても旅費を払うことができない貧しいヨーロッパ人たちが行っていた方法と事実上同じものである。しかしこのような自由意志による奴隷は奴隷として生きてゆくつもりはなかったので、マカオに到着すると直ちに大陸各地に逃亡するのが常であった。当然のことながらポルトガル人にとっては望ましい奴隷ではないのでその値段は非常に安価であった[32]。

　これら四つの原因のうちでも貧困によるものは特に注目しなければならない。領主たちに重税を課せられた農民たちはまったくの極貧となり、

自分たちを売るしかなかった[33]。つまり当時の日本の社会そのものが奴隷発生の原因をつくりだし、さらにはポルトガル人がそのような奴隷を買って海外に送り出すことを可能にしていたわけである。

秀吉の激怒

　カトリック教会のイエズス会に属するフランシスコ・ザビエルが1549年に鹿児島に上陸したとき、薩摩の領主は島津貴久であった。ザビエルは島津貴久から布教の許可を得てこの地域で布教活動を始めた。1551年にザビエルは後奈良天皇と将軍足利義輝から日本全国で布教をする許可を得ようとしたが果たせず、日本を去って中国大陸に渡った。ザビエルの後、ルイス・フロイスなどのカトリックの宣教師たちが渡来し、日本は次第にカトリックの影響を受けていくようになった。日本は戦国時代であり、武将の中でも特に織田信長が勢力を強め、足利家による将軍を廃止し、日本を支配する事実上の権力者となった。

　信長はヨーロッパに関することすべてに興味をいだいていたため、キリスト教に対しても敵対的ではなかった。従ってルイス・フロイスに宣教をする許可を与えた。その後信長が1582年に本能寺で劇的な非業の死をとげたのは周知のとおりである。この事件は日本史上よく知られている出来事であるにもかかわらず謎に満ちており、その真相は未だに不明である。数学者から歴史学者になった立花京子による膨大な資料の研究結果によれば、これにはイエズス会が暗躍しているとのことである。つまりイエズス会はキリスト教に好意的であった信長を利用してイエズス会の布教を成功させようとしたが信長が思惑通りに動かず、これに反発したイエズス会が暗殺してしまったというものである[34]。

　信長の後に日本一の権力者になった秀吉は最初は信長の政策を継承し、キリスト教に対しても敵対的ではなかった。しかしこの秀吉の態度は1587年に激変してしまった。この年、秀吉は九州征伐におもむき、そ

こで初めてポルトガル人が多数の日本人奴隷を海外に送り出していることを知ったのである。秀吉は激怒した。秀吉は奴隷の存在そのものには反対ではなかった。当時の日本で奴隷が存在していたことは秀吉もよく知っていた事実であった。秀吉が激怒した理由としていくつか考えられるが、そのひとつは日本人奴隷がポルトガル人によって牛馬のように扱われていたためである。

秀吉が九州平定のため出陣したときの旅の様子と行軍の記録は『九州御動座記』という名の文書として知られており、秀吉の側近であった大村由己の書いたものとされる文章の中にこのことが記されている。その一部を現代文の日本語で要約すると「後戸、平戸、長崎などに南蛮船が入港すると……数百人の男女が黒船に買い取られ、手足に鉄の鎖をつけられて船底に追い込まれ、地獄の苦しみよりひどいものである……」[35]とある。

当時の日本では、ガスパール・コエルホが1581年から1590年までイエズス会の支部長で、秀吉とコエルホは数回会談した経験があった。ところが1587年に平戸の港に停泊中であったポルトガル船にたまたま乗船していたコエルホは、突然秀吉の使者に呼び出され上陸するように命令された。そして使者はコエルホに面会するとただちに五箇条の詰問をした。その質問は現代文の日本語で書くと次のようなものである。

質問その1——コエルホとその同僚はいかなる権限のもとで秀吉の臣下をイエズス会の信者になるよう強制するのか。

質問その2——宣教師たちはなぜ弟子や信者たちをそそのかして神社仏閣を破壊させているのか。

質問その3——なぜ僧侶を迫害するのか。

質問その４――なぜイエスズ会とポルトガル人は耕作に必要な牛を食用にするのか。

質問その５――イエスズ会支部長コエルホはポルトガル人が日本人を買い入れ奴隷としてインドに送っているのをなぜ容認しているのか[36]。

この詰問の件はルイス・フロイスの記した 1588 年 2 月 20 日付の公式文書に明記されており[37]、同じくフロイス著の『日本史』にも述べられている[38]。この『日本史』によれば秀吉は「……日本に交易のためにやってくるポルトガル人その他が多くの人々を買い入れ、奴隷として船で本国に送っていると聞いている。これは自分にとって耐えられない。従って今日までにインドその他の遠隔地に売られていった日本人のすべてを日本に送り返すように努力していただきたい。遠隔であるために送り返すことが不可能であるならば、少なくとも現在ポルトガル人が買い入れた者を放免していただきたい。自分は奴隷を購入したときの費用を支払う用意がある」とも述べている[39]。秀吉はポルトガル人だけが日本人の奴隷を船で遠隔地に輸送しているのではないことは知っていた。しかしそれと共に秀吉は奴隷のほとんどはポルトガル人によって輸送されていたことも知っていた。そのため日本でのポルトガル人社会で指導的立場にあったコエルホに最初に問いただしたのである。

秀吉はこの問題を解決する決心をし、日本人奴隷の売買に関わった日本人は死刑にするという布令をだしており、事実これに違反して日本人をポルトガル船に運んだ罪で死刑に処せられた日本人もいた[40]。しかしこの布令はポルトガル人には適用されなかった[41]。ポルトガル人の場合には外交的な方法で警告されたり不明確な表現で注意されただけであった。例えばこの布令の後長崎奉行になった寺沢広高は外国人であっても違反者は厳しく罰せられるという告示をしている。しかしこの場合でも

死刑になるとは述べられていない[42]。

日本は似たような内容の外交文書をマカオ市やアジア各地のイエズス会司教に送付している[43]。しかし秀吉は布教と交易を明確に区別していた。秀吉はキリスト教は嫌ったものの、1592年の時点でさえ商人に成り変った宣教師が日本に残留することを認めている[44]。布教活動をしないことが条件であった。

ポルトガル側の態度と反応

これら一連の日本での出来事に対し、ポルトガルはどのような態度を示し、どのような反応を示したのであろうか。ポルトガルの国王ドン・セバスチアンは1571年3月12日付の勅令で日本人奴隷の売買を禁止した。これはポルトガル国王による一連の勅令の最初のものである。それによるとポルトガル人が日本人を捕えたり買ったりすることを禁止するとし、すでに奴隷にされた日本人は解放されなければならないと述べている。日本人を捕えたり買い取ったポルトガル人はその財産すべてを没収されるものとし、その半分はポルトガル王国の所有となり、残りの半分は告発した者に帰属する、と決められている[45]。

日本でのイエズス会は1596年に破門令をだし、奴隷売買にたずさわったポルトガル人は破門されると述べている[46]。翌1597年4月16日にはインド副王がポルトガル国王の名において第二回目の勅令を公にしている。この勅令によれば、奴隷であるかないかに関わらず、いかなる日本人でもマカオに到着したり居住することを強制されてはならないと定められている[47]。しかしこれに違反した場合の罰則は書かれていない。イエズス会は1598年に再び破門令を公布し、奴隷売買に従事した者は破門され、奴隷の少年または少女1人につき10クルゼーロの罰金を科せられる、としている[48]。最初の破門令の原文は現存しないため、そこに同一のまたは同様の罰則が記されていたかどうかは明らかでない。

1600年頃、ポルトガル国王は第三回目の勅令をだし、第一次と第二次の勅令の有効性を確認している[49]。

21世紀の常識で考えると、これらポルトガル国王とイエズス会による勅令や破門令は人道的、道徳的な配慮のために公布されたものと考えられるかもしれないが、現実はそうではなかった。これらの勅令と破門令はまったく異なった理由にもとづくものであった。

理由は二つある。第一に、アジア在住のポルトガル人の多くはカトリック教会の教えを無視し、日本人奴隷の女性と同棲して堕落した人生を過ごしていた。この問題はポルトガル人が書いた文書の中に何度も記載されている[50]。例えば1583年にマカオを出港してインドに向かっていた船がマラッカ海峡で遭難した時の様子をディオゴ・デ・コウトは次のように述べている。「神を恐れることなく、商人などが色白の美しい少女たちを妾とし、自分たちの船室の中で同棲している。神がそのような恥知らずの行動を罰したのは当然だ。神は大量の荷を積んだ船を失う損失を与え、神の偉大な力を理解させたのだ。世界の中でも、この地域のポルトガル人には淫猥な行為が特別に多く、目に余るものがある。その為に神が何度もの台風によってこのような人たちを威嚇し罰したのは明らかだ」[51]。

ガスパール・コエルホも秀吉がキリスト教を禁じた理由のひとつはポルトガル商人たちの不道徳ぶりであるとして次のように述べている。「これらの商人たちは若い人妻を奪い妾とし、子供を誘拐して船に連れ込み奴隷にしている。従ってその多くは自殺を選ぶ」[52]。ポルトガル人の不道徳ぶりは1598年のイエズス会の破門令にも指摘されている[53]。

第二に、ポルトガル人が日本と朝鮮半島から奴隷を安く買い取り商品として扱ったことによって、キリスト教に対する悪評が広まってしまったという理由があった。この問題は1599年2月20日付の日本のイエズス会からポルトガルのイエズス会支部長宛の手紙に明確に記されている[54]。つまり勅令と破門令の目的は日本のポルトガル人たちがこれ以上

堕落することを防ぎ、同時にキリスト教の悪評を防ぐことにあった。
　別の表現を用いると、日本のイエズス会は自らの存在の危機に直面したために奴隷売買に反対することを始めたのであった。日本のイエズス会はポルトガル人が日本で奴隷を買い入れ海外に売っていたことは充分に承知していた。そればかりではない。イエズス会は奴隷売買を大目に見ていただけではなく、それを公式に承認していた。1598年の二度目の破門令によれば、日本のイエズス会は日本人の少年と少女の奴隷の出荷の文書に署名をして公式の承認していた[55]。つまりイエズス会は奴隷売買を公式に認めていたのである。

奴隷売買禁止の効果

　日本とポルトガル双方の法令、勅令、破門令などにもかかわらず、奴隷取引の禁止には事実上効果はなかった。17世紀に至っても日本人奴隷が海外に送られていた文書が存在している[56]。1603年にゴア在住のポルトガル人がポルトガル国王宛に書いた奴隷売買についての陳情書がある。それによれば、ポルトガル国王による第一次の勅令には奴隷売買を廃止する効果はまったくなかったとしている[57]。この勅令を遵守する努力は妨害されてその存在など意識されていなかった。インド副王は勅令に従って任務をする役人の任命さえしていなかった[58]。インドやアジア各地に在住するポルトガル人は勅令を無視し、ポルトガル商人たちは何事もなかったかのように奴隷売買を継続していた。
　日本側にも二つの問題があった。第一に、領主は農民に極度の課税をしたため農民たちは自らを、そして家族を奴隷として売ることを余儀なくされていた。秀吉がコエルホに詰問した際、コエルホは一番大切なことは、奴隷を連れ去る外国船が入港する港を管理している領主がそのような船の入港を禁止することであると反論している[59]。
　第二に、1543年にポルトガル人が日本に鉄砲を持ち込んだ時、日本

は戦国時代であったという事実である。大名たちは直ちに鉄砲の有利さを理解しそれを戦で用い始めた。従って日本では急速に鉄砲の需要が高まり、堺、国友、根来、雑賀などで大量の鉄砲が生産されるようになった[60]。しかしここで戦国時代の大名にとって問題が発生した。戦で鉄砲を用いるには火薬が必要である。火薬を製造するには硝石が必要である。しかし当時の日本では硝石は資源として存在しなかったため日本国内で火薬を製造することができなかった。そのため、大名たちは輸入された火薬に頼るしかなかった。戦国大名にとっては安定した火薬の供給があるかないかは死活問題である。安定した火薬供給を確保するために洗礼を受けた大名さえ存在した[61]。

　火薬を買えばその支払いをしなければならない。支払いには奴隷を差し出した大名も現れた。ポルトガル国王ジョン3世は「火薬の樽1個に対し日本人は奴隷50人を提供した」と発言したとされている[62]。イエズス会は天草地方の三隅湾の海岸を「白銀海岸」と呼んでいたと言われている。その理由はここから奴隷が送り出され、硝石は銀色をしているからである[63]。

　奴隷の売買が禁止されることによって損害を受ける者は当然のこととして強硬に反対した。例えば奴隷売買を盛んに行っていたゴア在住のポルトガル人である。日本のイエズス会が1598年に奴隷売買に従事していると見なされた者を破門したことを知ると、これらのポルトガル人は1603年と1605年の二度にわたりポルトガル国王フィリーペ2世に抗議文の手紙を送っている。

　最初の抗議文は次のように述べている。「奴隷を解放することはインド在住のポルトガル人に莫大な損害をもたらすので我々は直ちに集会をし、いかにしてこの問題に対処すべきかについて話し合った。これまで我々は奴隷を買い入れるために百万クルゼーロ、またはそれ以上の出費をしている。しかも日本でのキリスト教を管理しているイエズス会の司教ならびに神父は公式の承認と許可の文書を発行することによって奴

隷を買い入れることを認めている。従って国王がこの事実を取り消して我々がすでに手に入れた奴隷を我々から奪うことを受け入れることはできない」[64]。

　この抗議文は次の事も述べている。「日本では日本人が公に売られて近隣のイスラムの国に送られイスラム信者になる。我々に買い取られた日本人はすべてキリスト教信者になり、これはポルトガル国王の臣民の数を増やすことになる。しかも彼らは我々の神父によって2年間の教育を受けた後、自由の身になる。インドに存在するポルトガル植民地には多くの日本人奴隷が存在する。非常時にはポルトガル人1人が5、6人の日本人奴隷にそれぞれ銃を持たせ率いることをすれば、日本人は非常に好戦的であるので我々にとって有利である。彼らが自由の身になっても我々の敵と協力して我々に反逆することはない。日本人奴隷の数は我々より少ないため我々を殺すようなことはしない」[65]。

　1605年の抗議文は次のように述べている。「ポルトガル国王による最初の勅令は過去30年間一度も実行に移されたことはなかった。インド在住のポルトガル副王はこの任務を遂行する役人を任命したことがない」[66]。そして次のようにも述べている。「奴隷たちは信頼関係にもとづいた契約に従って購入されたものであるので奴隷を解放するのは不当である。奴隷を購入するのに大金が費やされているので、もし奴隷が解放されれば奴隷所有者の中には千から二千クルゼーロもの損害を受ける者もあり、その数も多いであろう」[67]。

　国王フィリーペ2世は1605年の3月に勅令を出し、次のように述べている。「これまでに公にされた勅令は広く適用される意味合いのものとなり、これは信頼関係にもとづいて合法的に所有されている奴隷にまで適用されることとなった。これはインド在住者に好ましくない形の影響を及ぼすこととなり、日本人奴隷をすべて解放することは重大な経済的被害を与えることになるという報告を受けている。合法的でもっともな理由がある場合には日本人奴隷の所有を禁じるつもりはない。これ

は前任者のドン・セバスチアン国王の意図でもあった。ゴア市やコチン市からの報告も受けているので事を明白にするために新しく勅令を公示することにした。もし日本人奴隷が法律に反して間違った理由で奴隷とされていると主張した場合にはその主張を検討し、法を遵守するために解放する努力をせよ。この件に関しては自分は神を信じ、自分に仕えるものの判断を信ずる」[68]。

国王フィリーペ２世の意図を要約すれば、もし法的で理由のある説明をすることができる場合には奴隷は所有してもよく、すべての奴隷を無条件に解放するのは自分の意図するところではない、前任の国王ドン・セバスチアンも同様に考えていたのだ、ということである。

奴隷売買の禁止が失敗した理由

これまでに述べた事項を要約すると下記の五項目にまとめることができる。第一に、日本人がなぜポルトガル人によって奴隷として売買されたのか。第二に、日本社会になぜ奴隷を生み出す背景があったのか。第三に、ポルトガル国王その他のポルトガル関係者がどのように奴隷問題に対応したのか。第四に、日本在住のイエズス会のポルトガル人がこの問題をどのように扱ったのか。そして第五に、アジア各地に在住のポルトガル人が奴隷売買を禁止する試みにどのように反応したのか、である。これらの歴史上の出来事を考察してみると、奴隷売買を禁止する努力は完全に失敗したと言わざるをえない。

その理由はしごく簡単に一言で表現できる。つまり、この問題に関与した関係者はすべて自身の個人的な利害関係を計算にいれて考え、発言し、行動していたためである。当時の日本では、領主は農民たちに極度の重税を課すことができたため、領主たちはそれを実行し続けた。これによって農民には選択の余地はなく、その犠牲者となり、自らまたは自らの家族を奴隷として売ることを余儀なくされた。戦国時代の大名た

ちは生き残って勝つために鉄砲を必要とし、輸入された火薬を必要としたのでその支払いに奴隷をあてることさえした。ポルトガルの植民地在住のポルトガル人は安い労働力とセックスを必要とし、成人男女ならびに少年少女を求めた。この条件にかなった奴隷が日本に存在していたので当然のことながらこれらの奴隷を買い入れた。商人としてみれば奴隷売買の仕事をすることによって金儲けができると知れば、これも当然ながらその仕事に従事することになる。その他にもポルトガル人は人攫いをして奴隷を手にいれていた。

　日本在住のイエズス会のポルトガル人たちはやはり日本在住の同国人の利害関係の主張を聞き、ポルトガル国とポルトガル人に有利な形で行動するようになる。その結果、場合によっては奴隷売買を支持することにもなる。しかしそれと同時に、イエズス会としては日本でできるだけ多くの改宗者を獲得し、その勢力を強めることが最大の目標である。それには日本人の間にイエズス会、ポルトガル国、ポルトガル人への敵対心が高まる危険性は絶対に回避しなければならない。

　このような矛盾した現実に対処するためにイエズス会としては奴隷売買に反対をしている印象を与え、その反面それを大目に見ていた。秀吉が激怒し日本人奴隷を解放せよ、と要求するにいたってイエズス会は日本の敵となる危険性に気がついた。秀吉の激怒に対処するためにイエズス会はポルトガル国王に奴隷売買禁止の陳情書を送り、破門令も公布した。しかし公布、布令、破門令、規則などが紙の上に書かれていることと、それが実行されることとは全く別の問題である。これは誰もが知っていた。奴隷売買は何事もなかったように継続していた。

　ポルトガル国王の立場からすると、このような国際間の問題に巻き込まれるのは好ましくなく面倒である。それを避ける一番安易な方法は、中身のない抽象的な文書を出し、直接関係している下部の人間たちに処理させることである。この問題すべてをまとめて考察すると時代や文化に無関係な、いつでも、どこにでも見られる人間のエゴイズムとして要

約できる。これは誰もが自らの利益と安全を考えるだけの歴史であった。そしてここでの犠牲者は不幸にも奴隷になってしまった日本人の成人男女と少年少女であった。

日本側の行動

1587年に秀吉は新たな規則を定め、大名がキリスト教に改宗する場合には秀吉の許可が必要になった。現実にはこれは大名がキリスト教信者にはなれないことを意味した。明石城主の高山右近はこれに違反したとして領地を没収された[69]。秀吉はさらに1587年7月25日に宣教師の国外退去を命ずるバテレン追放令を定めた[70]。

1596年にはいわゆる「サン＝フェリーペ号事件」が起こった。これは土佐沖で遭難したスペイン船サン＝フェリーペ号の乗組員が「スペインが植民地を形成するとき、まず宣教師を送り込み、土地の住民たちを手なずけ、その次に軍隊を送り込んで植民地としてしまうのだ」と発言したことになっている[71]。すべての南蛮人を疑いの目で眺めていた秀吉はこの報告を受けて直ちに行動した。宣教師と改宗した日本人信者が逮捕され、同じ年の1596年に長崎で処刑された。

これは広く知られた事件であるにもかかわらず、その詳細については情報源によってかなり異なる。カトリック教会はこの事件を重大に受けとめ、これを絵画に残している。しかしイエズス会の描いた絵画には単に3人のイエズス会所属者しか描かれていない。フランシスコ会の描いたものにはイエズス会所属者は描かれておらず、単に23人のフランシスコ会所属者のみが描かれている。唯一の例外を除き、処刑された者全員の絵画は存在しない[72]。カトリック教会は1862年にこの犠牲者を聖人と認めたがその数は26人となっている。

日本側の情報もいろいろあり、6人のフランシスコ会の宣教師と20人の日本人信者とされていたり[73]、6人のフランシスコ会所属者、3人

のイエズス会所属者、19人の日本人信者となっていたりする[74]。単にカトリックの宣教師と言っても、当時の日本には少なくともイエズス会、フランシスコ会、ドミニカ会、アウガスティン会の宣教師が存在していたことが知られており、しかもこれらの異なった会派の間の睨み合いと争いがあったことも知られているので、それが原因である可能性が高い[75]。

この事件によって日本とスペインの関係は悪化した。秀吉の後、将軍となり事実上日本一の権力者となった家康はこの事態に配慮した。当時の東アジアでスペインの植民地勢力の中心地はルソンで、家康はルソンに外交使節を送っている。徳川幕府は1610年にも京都の商人田中勝介をスペイン領であるメキシコに派遣し、メキシコとの交易をすすめることを試みた。これは千葉に漂着したスペイン船に便乗した試みであったが失敗に終わっている。

1612年にはキリスト教の全面的禁止となった。キリスト教の教会は破壊され、幕府直轄の領地内から宣教師は追放された。1613年にはこれが全国にまで拡大され禁教令として施行された。

禁教令施行の後、徳川幕府の態度はさらに強硬になっていった。1614年にはキリスト教からの改宗を拒否した高山右近を含め、300人がルソンに追放となった。1616年には中国船以外の外国船は平戸と長崎以外に入港することを禁止された。1629年頃には信者摘発の方法として踏絵が実行されはじめた。

1636年には日本在住のポルトガル人は長崎の出島に隔離され、1638年にはキリスト教は厳禁という形で完全禁止となった。1639年にはポルトガル船は日本の港すべてに入港することを禁止され、この時点でポルトガルとスペインは日本から完全に閉め出されることになった。奴隷売買に関与していなかったイギリスも日本から閉め出された。オランダ人は例外とされたヨーロッパ人であったが、それでも1641年に出島に隔離されることになり、一般にこの年が鎖国の始まりとされている。

ヨーロッパ各国が日本と接触を始めた後、日本側の方針としては交易

と宣教活動を区別していた。そのためキリスト教が禁じられても交易は続けられた。すでに述べられたように、宣教師と日本人信者が長崎で処刑されたが、その後にスペインの植民地であるメキシコと交易をする試みをしている。そして日本はスペインやポルトガルのようなカトリックの国とオランダやイギリスのような非カトリックの国をはっきりと区別していた。しかしこの二種類の国々がお互いに攻撃し中傷しあっていたことを日本側でも承知していた[76]。そのため日本はどちらの側からも反対側の国々の危険性やそれに似たような噂をたえず聞かされていた。従って日本にとってもっとも納得のゆく合理的な判断は、ヨーロッパの国すべてを疑いの目でながめることであった。カトリックであるかないかに関わらず、キリスト教の国はすべて危険であると見なすのが最も安全である。従って日本にとっての最善策は鎖国を選ぶことであった。

これらの出来事の解釈

歴史上の出来事を取り上げ、それらの出来事が別の形で処理されていたらとか、ある特定の事件が起こらなかったら、などと仮定し、その場合歴史はどのように展開していただろうか、などと考えるのは大いに興味があるものの、実際には全く意味のないことである。16世紀の終わりに秀吉が日本の権力者として現れ、あのように決断し行動していなかったらと考えても意味がない。歴史は歴史である。にもかかわらず、最小限度の推測が許されるとすれば、秀吉が現れなかったら日本はカトリックの国になっていたかもしれないし、カトリックとプロテスタントの間の熾烈な憎みあい殺しあいが日本で再現されていたかもしれない。信長は仏教に反対の態度をとったばかりかそれを行動にあらわすことによってキリスト教が広まることを助けた[77]と言えるので、その意味でもこの信長と秀吉両者の違いが歴史に反映されているとも言える。

秀吉の観点からすれば、奴隷売買そのものは容認されることであった。これは秀吉の時代の日本では事実であった。秀吉が激怒した理由はポルトガル人たちが事実上の日本の支配者でしかも最高の権力者を無視し、その許可も得ずに勝手に行動していたことにあった。日本奴隷を海外に勝手に輸送していただけではない。神社仏閣は破壊し、農業用の牛を屠殺して食用とし、仏教の僧侶を迫害し、日本人にキリスト教に改宗することを強制している、などといったポルトガル人たちの目に余る行動の情報が耳に入れば、事実上の国家元首と自負していた秀吉が激怒し、それなりに行動したのももっともと言える。それだけではない。日本人奴隷は牛馬同様に鎖につながれ船底に追いやられて輸送されていたことは、すでに引用された側近の大村由己の書いた文章の口調からも推測できるように、日本人の考える奴隷の扱い方より非人道的で、「地獄よりひどい」ものであったのは確かである。
　海外に送られた奴隷が数年後には自由の身になれた可能性は大いにありうる。しかしここにも問題がある。日本国内での奴隷であれば何といっても日本文化の中での生活であり、自由になった場合には生まれ故郷に帰る可能性も充分ある。しかし海外に送られた奴隷の場合には、いくら自由の身になっても日本に帰るなどということは事実上不可能である。このようないろいろの理由が総合的に考慮された結果が秀吉の具体的行動として実行されたものと思われる。
　ポルトガル側の口先だけで行動を伴わない態度は、日本側に不信と疑惑と敵意の反応をもたらすには充分すぎるものであった。この態度では日本に決定的な行動をとらせることになっても少しも不思議ではない。そしてサン＝フェリーペ号事件がその引き金となった。そしてその後の鎖国に至るまでの一連の行動もすべてこの観点から理解されるべきである。

結論

　日本は 1641 年に鎖国政策を実行し始め、外国との接触を最小限に保つことによって、元禄文化のようなある意味では日本独自の文化を形成し発展することができた。資本主義の始まりのような経済も発展した。鎖国には好ましくない点もあったと議論するのは容易である。しかし徳川幕府支配の日本は戦国時代とは異なり、原則的には平和であり、なによりも問題を起こし続けた厄介なヨーロッパ人たちを排除できたことは日本に有利であった。

　ちょうどこの理由のために 1853 年に黒船が渡来し、開国を迫り、あらゆる手段を用いて脅迫した時、日本はまったくその必要を感じなかった。日本側の明確な拒否のため、アメリカはその軍事力と技術力を徹底的に誇示し、もし日本にその気がないのなら、アメリカは日本を攻撃し、どちらが勝つか決めてみせる、と威嚇し脅迫した[78]。軍事力と技術力ではアメリカにはるかに劣ると見せ付けられた日本はアメリカのいいなりになり、開国に無理やりに同意させられたのである。

　これは日本にとって屈辱的で憤懣やるかたない出来事で、幕府を代表し、老中首座としてアメリカ側と交渉した阿部正弘はその怒りと悔しさを「血の涙が出るほどだ」と記録にのこしている[79]。福沢諭吉は、開国の仕事にあたった徳川幕府の人間たちは、心の中では外国人たちを徹底的に憎み嫌っていた[80]と述べている。

　この黒船に始まった開国は日本にとっては屈辱であり、苦痛であり、怒りであり、トラウマであり、何よりも極度の憤懣であった。軍事力と技術力が劣っていたためにこのような惨めさと哀れさを味合わされたと理解した日本は「西洋化」と「近代化」に励むことになった。その背景にあったものは、憎い西洋に打ち勝つには西洋の軍事力と技術力を手に入れなければならないという思想があったためである[81]。

その結果日本は「西洋化」と「近代化」に成功し、日清・日露戦争に勝ち、第一次世界大戦でも戦勝国の一つとなり、世界でばかにされない一流国になったと思っていたところ、西洋は人種主義によって日本を攻撃することを始めた。これは日本にとって新しく現れた別の形の西洋に対する憤懣と怒りであった。真珠湾攻撃はこの観点から理解すべきである[82]。このように考えるとポルトガル人による日本人奴隷売買は反西洋という一連の事柄の最初の出来事であると見なすことができる。別の表現を用いると、一個人、組織、国などの違いに関係なく、人間の行動は常に予期しなかった結果を生み出す可能性を含んでおり、場合によっては戦争のような大事件にさえなりうるという解釈もできる[83]。

注ならびに文献

1 　一説によれば、1541年にポルトガル船が九州の臼杵に漂着したとされている。鬼塚英昭「皇室に封印された聖書」(『天皇のロザリオ(下)』)、成甲書房、2006年、90ページ、参照。
2 　岡本良知『十六世紀日欧交通史の研究(改訂増補)』、原書房、1974年、570、728ページ。
3 　柳田利夫「海を渡った日本人奴隷」『朝日百科・世界の歴史』69巻、1990年、D438ページ。
4 　郡司喜一『十七世紀に於ける日暹関係』、外務省調査部、1934年、534ページ。
5 　Satow, Ernest, "Note on the Intercourse between Japan and Siam in the Seventeenth Century," *Transactions of the Asiatic Society of Japan,* Vol. 13, 1885, p.182.
6 　郡司、前掲書、534ページ。
7 　Guerreiro, Fernão, *Relação Anual das Coisas que Fizeram os Padres da Companhia de Jesus,* II. (Coimbra: Impr. Da Universidade,1930), p.312.
8 　*Ibid.,* p. 312.
9 　郡司、前掲書、537ページ。
10 　岡本、前掲書、778ページ。
11 　柳田、前掲書、D438ページ。
12 　大塚真琴「演説館　ラテンアメリカに於ける日本人自由渡航民の顛末」『三田評論』2000年3月号、72-5ページ。
13 　井上満郎他『理解しやすい日本史B』文英堂、1995年、163ページ。
14 　同上。
15 　『デ・サンデ天正遣欧使節記』、泉井久之助他訳、雄松堂書店、1969年、233ページ。
16 　大塚、前掲書、73ページ。
17 　『高麗史』28巻、1452年。
18 　井上他、前掲書、132ページ。
19 　秋山謙蔵「『倭寇』による朝鮮・支那人奴隷の掠奪とその送還及び売買」『社会経済史学会』第2巻8号、1932年、811-839ページ。
20 　岡本、前掲書、766ページ。

21 同上、730 ページ。
22 Barros, João de, *Da Asia, Nova Edição*. (originally Lisboa, 1778; Coimbra: Impr. Da Universidade, 1932), Dec.III, Liv., Cap. II.
23 Pagés, Leon, *Histoire de la religion chrétienne au Japon depuis 1598 jusqu'a 1651,* II.(Paris:C. Douniol,1869-70), p. 72, 73.
24 Frois, Luis, *Apparatos para a Historia Ecclestiastica do Bispado de Japão.* (Lisboa, 1812), fl. 267v.
25 岡本、前掲書、763 ページ。
26 Storck, Wilhelm, *Vida e Obras de Luis Camões*. (Lisboa: Academia Real das Sciencias, 1898), pp. 586, 652.
27 岡本、前掲書、757-764 ページ。
28 Pagés, *op. cit.*, II, pp. 72-74.
29 *Ibid.*, pp. 73, 74.
30 *Ibid.*, pp. 74, 75; Frois, *op. cit.*, I, fl. 495; *op. cit.*, II, fls. 23v, 24.
31 Pagés, *op. cit.*, II, pp. 74, 75.
32 *Ibid.*, pp. 74, 75.
33 Avila Girón, Bernardino, "Relación del Reino del Nippon," *Archivo Ibero-Americano*, Año XXI, No.113, p.34; Frois, *op. cit.*, II, fls. 23v, 24; *op. cit.*, I, fl. 495.
34 立花京子『信長と十字架』、集英社、2004 年。
35 『九州御動座記』、1587 年。全文が清水紘一『織豊政権とキリシタン』、岩田書店、2001 年、405 ページに掲載されている。
36 徳富猪一郎『近世日本国民史豊臣時代 乙』、民友社、1920 年、379-380 ページ。
37 *Cartas qve os Padres e Irmãos de Companhia de Iesus escreuerão dos Reynos de Iapão & China aos da mesma Companhia da India, & Europa, desdo anno de 1549, até o de 1580.* (Evora, 1598), II, fl. 108.
38 Frois, *op. cit.*, I.; Frois, Luis, *Historia do Japão,* edição anotada por Jose Wicki. (Lisboa: Biblioteca Nacional, 1776); ルイス・フロイス『日本史』全 12 巻、松田毅一他訳、中央公論社、1978-9 年。
39 Frois, *op. cit.*, 1776, fl. 481.
40 Pagés, *op. cit.*, pp. 73, 76.
41 岡本、前掲書、740 ページ。
42 同上。
43 同上、741 ページ。

44 柳田利夫「豊臣秀吉インド副王宛書簡案文について」『ビブリア』88号、1987年5月、55-59ページ。
45 de J. H. Da Cunha Rivara, Ed., *Archivo Portuguez-Oriental*. (Nova-Goa, 1857-1875), Fusc. V, Pt. II, pp. 791, 792.
46 この件そのものについての文献は現存しないが、その内容は1598年の文献から推察が可能である。
47 de J. H. Da Cunha Rivara, *op. cit.*, Fusc. III, pp. 763, 764.
48 Pagés, *op. cit.*, p. 71.
49 de J. H. Da Cunha Rivara, *op. cit.*, Fusc. I, Pt. II, p. 125.
50 Ayres, Christovao, *Fernao Mendes Pinto*. (Lisboa, 1905), p.89.
51 Couto, Diogo de, *Da Asia*. (originally 1602-1645; Lisboa: Na Regia Officina Typografica, 1777-1788), dec. X, liv. III, Cap. XIV.
52 Delplace, Louis, *S.Francois-Xavier et ses premiers successeurs, 1540-43 (Le Catholicisme au Japon,* I), (Bruxelles: Libr. Albert Dewit, 1909).
53 Pagés, *op. cit.*, II, p. 76.
54 井澤實「通商秘話（日本人輸出考）」『東京朝日新聞』1932年7月11日。
55 Pagés, *op. cit.*, II, p. 71.
56 徳富、前掲書、748ページ。
57 de J. H. Cunha Rivara, *op. cit.*, Fasc. I, Pt. II, p. 125.
58 *Ibid.*, Fasc.I, Pt. II. pp. 125, 127.
59 Frois, *op. cit.*, I, fl. 481.
60 井上他、前掲書、160ページ。
61 鬼塚、前掲書、107ページ、110ページ。
62 同上、117ページ。
63 同上、106、107、110ページ。
64 de J. H. da Cunha Rivara, *op. cit.*, Fasc. I, Pt. II, pp. 125, 126.
65 *Ibid*, Fasc. I, Pt. II, p. 127.
66 *Ibid.*, Fasc. I, Pt. II, p. 157.
67 *Ibid.*, Fasc. I, Pt. II, p. 157.
68 *Documentos Remetidos da India ou Livros das Monções*. (Lisboa:Publicação da Academia Real das Sciencias de Lisboa, 1883-1893), p. 43; 高瀬弘一郎訳注『モンスーン文書と日本――十七世紀ポルトガル公文書集』、八木書店、2006年、131-132ページ。

69　井上他、前掲書、168 ページ。
70　徳富、前掲書、388-9 ページ。
71　徳富、前掲書、21 ページ。井上他、前掲書、168 ページ。これは通説とされているが 松田毅一は疑問視をしている。松田毅一『秀吉の南蛮外交』、新人物往来社、1972 年、278 ページ、参照。
72　宮崎賢太郎「キリシタン時代におけるイエズス会日本管区の人的構成と評価について」、箭内健次編『鎖国日本と国際交流(上巻)』、吉川弘文館、1988 年、81 ページ。
73　徳富、前掲書、22 ページ。
74　鬼塚、前掲書、102 ページ。
75　宮崎、前掲書、80、81 ページ。
76　井上他、前掲書、191 ページ。
77　立花、前掲書、175 ページ。
78　Kitahara, Michio, *Children of the Sun*. (New York: St. Martin's Press, 1989), Chapters 2, 3.
79　中根雪江『昨夢紀事』(1853-1858 年) 第 1 巻、日本史籍協会編、東京大学出版会、1920 年、159 ページ。
80　福沢諭吉『福翁自伝』(1899 年)、『福沢諭吉全集』、岩波書店、1959 年、147-8 ページ。
81　Kitahara, Michio, "The Rise of Four Mottoes in Japan," *Journal of Asian History*, Vol. 20, No. 1, 1986, pp. 54-57; Kitahara, Michio, *op. cit.*, Chapters 4, 5, 6.
82　北原惇『なぜ太平洋戦争になったのか』、ＴＢＳブリタニカ、2001 年。
83　いわゆる「オーストリア学派」に属する経済学者や哲学者は、人間の行動から発生するまったく予期しない結果の重要性を強調する。この点については下記の文献などを参考にされたい。　Menger, Carl, *Investigations into the Method of the Social Sciences with Special Reference to Economics*, (New York: New York University Press, 1985), pp. 139-59; and Mises, Ludwig von, *Human Action*. (Chicago: Henry Regnery, 1966), pp. 92-118.

PORTUGUESE COLONIALISM

AND

JAPANESE SLAVES

PORTUGUESE COLONIALISM AND JAPANESE SLAVES

Michio Kitahara

Kadensha Tokyo

Portuguese Colonialism
and
Japanese Slaves

 This is a much revised and expanded version of *Naze Taiheiyo Senso ni Nattanoka* (Why Did the Pacific War Break Out?) by Jun Kitahara, Chapter 1, (Tokyo: TBS-Britannica, 2001). Jun Kitahara is Michio Kitahara's pen name when he publishes in Japanese.

First published 2013
by Kadensha, Shuppan Yuso Bldg., 2F
2-5-11 Nishi-Kanda
Chiyoda-ku, Tokyo, Japan 101-0065

kadensha@muf.biglobe.ne.jp
http://kadensha.net

ⓒ Michio Kitahara 2013

All rights reserved. No part of this publication may be reproduced or transmitted in any form or by any means without prior permission in writing from the publishers, except for short extracts in criticism.

Contents

Preface 7

Portuguese Colonialism and Japanese Slaves

Introduction 11
Japanese Slaves Overseas 11
The Reasons Why Some Japanese Became Slaves 14
The Rise of Hideyoshi and His Fury 15
Portuguese Attitudes and Responses 18
The Effect of the Prohibition of Slavery 20
The Reasons Why the Abolition of the Slave Trade Failed 24
Japanese Actions 25
An Interpretation of the Incidents 29
Conclusion 30

Notes 32

Preface

In order to understand the history of a country and its people, it is necessary to gather as much information as possible, and, above all, to study the most important events that have taken place in its history. In reality, it may be impossible to gather all the information about a country over a long period of time. We must accept the limitations of human capability and human knowledge.

But at the same time, it is totally objectionable to exclude historical facts that must be taken into account. Whether or not this exclusion is accidental or intentional is not important. Whichever is the case, the result is an incorrect or biased history of the country that we are trying to study.

Unfortunately, this is the case when the West tries to study the history of Japan. The purpose of the paper that follows is to discuss a series of events that are essential in understanding Japanese history. This paper may reveal events that are totally unknown, incredible, and unpleasant to read. Nevertheless, in the ongoing quest to advance our knowledge about Japan and its history, this paper can hopefully provide a positive contribution as well.

When I published the book entitled *Children of the Sun* in 1989 (New York: St. Martin's Press), I did not include this topic due to several practical reasons, and I later regretted this decision greatly. I sincerely hope the reader will gain a better picture of Japan and its history by reading the paper that follows.

Portuguese Colonialism
and
Japanese Slaves

Introduction

The relative isolation of Japan from the rest of the world changed dramatically when Europe entered the age of colonialism. In 1543, a Chinese ship with Portuguese on board accidentally drifted to the island of Tanegashima; this event is generally considered to be the first contact between Japan and Europe.[1] It was on this occasion that the Portuguese introduced firearms to the Japanese. This was the beginning of Japan's trade with the West. As the fact that Portuguese traders were on a Chinese ship indicates, trade between Japan and Portugal included Chinese products; in fact, most of the products that the Portuguese sold to the Japanese were Chinese products, such as silk and spices. But along with this kind of trade came a more insidious type of trade that is little-known both in Japan and in the rest of the world even to this day---the Portuguese sold Japanese slaves overseas.

Japanese Slaves Overseas

Toward the end of the 16th century, a large number of Japanese were in several parts of Asia. But there was little information about the Japanese leaving Japan. This was because most of these overseas Japanese were shipped as slaves instead of traveling as free individuals.[2] They were found in the regions where Portugal was dominant as a colonial power, such as India, southeast Asia, and southern China, particularly in Macao, around the Strait of Malacca, and in Goa, India.[3]

When Siam fought a war against Burma and Laos in 1585 and

1587, there were Japanese in the Siamese Army.[4] Satow states that when Siam was invaded by Burma and Laos in 1579, there were 500 Japanese soldiers in the Siamese Army,[5] but Gunji thinks this refers to the war of 1585 or 1587.[6] In 1605, a British ship commanded by John Davis fought Japanese pirates at Pata on the Malay Peninsula, and both the pirates and Davis were killed.[7] In 1606, 11 ships led by Dutch admiral Cornelius Mateleif attacked the Portuguese colony of Malacca, and Japanese soldiers fought together with the Portuguese, forcing the Dutch to retreat.[8] When civil war broke out in Siam in 1610, 280 Japanese soldiers fought on the rebel side, occupying the city of Ayutthaya and forcing the king to yield to various demands.[9] Okamoto thinks these Japanese were originally slaves brought into these regions in the 16th century.[10]

Historical documents show that Japanese slaves could be found even in Portugal[11] and Argentina.[12] Christianity was introduced to Japan in 1549 by Francisco Xavier, a Jesuit missionary, and by 1582, there were approximately 145,000 converted Japanese Christians.[13] Some of them were feudal lords, and three of them, Ohtomo Sorin, Arima Harunobu, and Ohmura Sumitada, decided to send four converted boys to the Pope in Rome in 1582. They carried out this mission by accepting the recommendation by Alexandro Valignano, an Italian missionary.[14] The boys traveled via Goa and Lisbon, met Pope Gregory XIII, and returned to Japan safely in 1590. This very unusual experience by the four Japanese boys was published in 1590 as *De Missione Legatorum Iaponen.*

In this publication, one of the boys named Michael states that he personally observed Japanese slaves at various places during his trip and became angry with the Japanese who had sold their fellow countrymen cheaply into slavery. Another boy named Martinus says he saw so many men, women, boys, and girls of his race in so many places around the world, many of whom had been sold cheaply and were engaging in miserable work.[15]

In the city of Cordoba, Argentina, there is an old institution called *Museo Histórico Provincial,* founded in 1574. The archives of this museum contain an extremely valuable document from 1597. According to this document, on March 4, 1597, a Japanese named Francisco Xapon filed a lawsuit to the court, insisting on three things. First, he states he is not a slave; second, he claims there is no justifiable reason for him to be sold and bought; and third, he states that he therefore must be freed. The court accepted his plea and he was freed in 1598.[16]

However, the Portuguese were not the only slave traders, nor were the Japanese the only victims. History was not that simple. Even before the arrival of the Portuguese, slavery existed in Asia, and slaves originated from two or more countries. In 1274, the combined forces of the Mongols, Chinese, Manchu, and Koreans invaded the Japanese island of Iki and massacred many Japanese. Two hundred Japanese children were captured, sent to Korea, and offered to the king and queen of the Goryeo Kingdom as slaves. Koreans themselves describe this in an official document.[17]

Pirates called *wako*, based on the Japanese islands of Tsushima and Iki as well as the Matsura region of Kyushu, were active from the mid-14th century. These pirates were mostly Japanese, but some were Koreans as well.[18] They sold Chinese and Korean slaves.[19] Japanese nationals were also sold to the Chinese and Indo-Chinese. [20] The Chinese sold Chinese slaves to traders on foreign ships.[21]

Portuguese were already involved in trading Chinese slaves as early as 1520.[22] Toward the end of the 16th century, a large number of Korean slaves were shipped to Japan and sold to the Portuguese together with Japanese slaves. Most of these Koreans became slaves after Japan's invasion of Korea in 1592 and 1597 and were transported by Portuguese ships coming from China.[23] Frois states Japanese soldiers captured Korean children.[24] Merchants in Nagasaki were most likely involved in the slave trade of Koreans.[25] Javanese slaves were very cheap and were shipped to Lisbon.[26]

The Reasons Why Some Japanese Became Slaves

There are four major reasons why the Japanese became slaves.[27] First, some Japanese forcibly captured other Japanese in a different feudal area of jurisdiction. These slaves were sold to the Portuguese, validated by the false claim that these Japanese were prisoners of war. It was possible to make such a transaction because the Jesuits from Portugal condoned using prisoners of war as slaves. In reality, there were not many prisoners of war in Japan at that time, and kidnapped Japanese became victims.[28]

Second, some became slaves as a result of the Japanese customs of the time. For example, when a man received the death penalty, his wife and children were forced to become slaves. A wife who refused to live with her husband, a son who deserted his father, or a servant who disliked his master and sought refuge under a feudal lord became a slave. When a man could not pay back a debt, his child or parent was sold as a slave.[29]

Third, because of poverty, parents might sell a child as a slave.[30] Fourth, a Japanese man who wanted to leave the country voluntarily sold himself as a slave.[31] This is similar to the indentured servitude widely adopted by poor Europeans as a way to emigrate to America.

However, according to Pagés, most of the Japanese were not prepared to live as slaves, and when they arrived at Macao, they fled to various destinations in China. Thus, from the Portuguese point of view, they were not desirable slaves and therefore cheap.[32]

It is important to note the emergence of slavery due to poverty. When feudal lords carried out an extremely harsh policy of taxation upon peasants, these peasants often became extremely poor, and there was no alternative but to sell themselves.[33] Thus, Japanese society itself created the possibility for the Portuguese to buy Japanese nationals and later sell them as slaves overseas.

The Rise of Hideyoshi and His Fury

When Francisco Xavier of the Jesuit Order arrived at Kagoshima on the island of Kyushu in 1549, the feudal lord administering this region was Shimazu Takahisa. He granted Xavier permission to engage in missionary activities there. In 1551, Xavier tried to gain permission for activities across the entire nation, both from Emperor Gonara and Shogun Ashikaga Yoshiteru, but he failed to meet them. Xavier left Japan in 1551, but other Catholic missionaries such as Luis Frois arrived. Japan was in a state of constant civil war at that time, and a powerful and rising feudal lord named Oda Nobunaga, who gradually became *de facto* head of the state, abolished the shogunate held by the Ashikaga family.

Nobunaga was interested in European culture, including Christianity, and he granted Luis Frois permission to engage in missionary work. But Nobunaga was assassinated in 1582. This was one of the most dramatic assassinations in Japanese history and is still shrouded in mystery. There is even speculation based on extensive research that Jesuits were involved. According to Tachibana, the Jesuits took advantage of Nobunaga's influence to spread their order, but when they gradually came to realize that Nobunaga could not be manipulated as they wanted, they assassinated him.[34] After this assassination, Toyotomi Hideyoshi took over the position of *de facto* head of the state.

At first, Hideyoshi continued Nobunaga's policy and was tolerant of Christianity. However, he changed his attitude toward it drastically in 1587. When he travelled to Kyushu in order to quell hostile feudal lords, he learned for the first time that the Portuguese were actively engaging in a slave trade in which Japanese slaves were being shipped overseas. He became furious. He was not against slavery itself; slavery already existed in Japan. He became furious because Japanese were being shipped like beasts overseas, among other reasons.

Hideyoshi's subordinate named Ohmura Yuki described the situation as follows: "...at the Goto Islands, Hirato, Nagasaki, and other places, ships of the southern barbarians (*nanban sen*) are influencing regional lords and our laws negatively. Not only that, these ships buy hundreds of Japanese men and women. Their hands and feet are chained, and they are driven into the bottom of the ships. This is far beyond the punishment in Hell... ."[35]

In 1587, Hideyoshi's representative questioned Gaspar Coelho, a priest who held the official position of Vice Provincial of the Jesuit Order in Japan between 1581 and 1590. He had five questions. Question 1: Under whose authority are you and your associates forcing Hideyoshi's subjects to become Christians? Question 2: Why are missionaries and others leading their disciples and believers to demolish Shinto shrines and Buddhist temples? Question 3: Why are you threatening Buddhist priests? Question 4: Why do you and other

Portuguese eat the cattle that we need for our agriculture? Question 5: Why is Vice Provincial Coelho allowing Portuguese nationals to buy Japanese and to export them as slaves to India? [36]

This inquiry was described in a document dated February 20, 1588, written by Luis Frois,[37] as well as in his *Historia de Japam*. [38] Hideyoshi also stated, "I have been informed that the Portuguese and others are buying many people [in Japan] and shipping them as slaves to their home countries. This is unbearable to me. Therefore I ask Father to try hard to return all Japanese sold to India and other distant places back to Japan. If this becomes impossible due to the geographical distances to these countries, at least free those who have been bought and are currently held by the Portuguese. I am prepared to pay the expenses already spent on such transactions." [39] Hideyoshi knew well that the Portuguese were not the only people who were shipping Japanese as slaves. But he also knew that the Portuguese were playing a dominant role in the slave trade. He contacted Coelho due to his influential position in the Portuguese community in Japan.

Hideyoshi was determined to solve this problem. He made a law stipulating the death penalty to any Japanese who had been involved in selling or buying Japanese slaves. Indeed, there were Japanese who were executed for arranging the transportation of Japanese to a Portuguese ship.[40] However, this law did not apply to the Portuguese.[41] They were warned through diplomacy or merely threatened in vague terms. For example, Terazawa Hirotaka, who became the *bugyo* (magistrate) in Nagasaki after this law was implemented, made an official announcement in writing, stating that anyone, including foreign nationals, who violates the anti-slavery law shall be severely punished, without mentioning the death penalty.[42] Japan also sent diplomatic documents of similar content to the City of Macao and to

Jesuit Bishops in various Asian cities.[43]

However, Hideyoshi made a distinction between religion and trade. He disliked Christians, but interestingly enough, he permitted some missionaries to stay on in Japan as merchants as late as in 1592,[44] as long as they did not engage in missionary activities.

Portuguese Attitudes and Responses

How did Portugal react to the fact that its colonists were actively involved in the trade of Japanese slaves? King Don Sebastian of Portugal issued a decree dated March 12, 1571, prohibiting the trade of Japanese slaves. This was the first of a series of decrees dealing with this matter. According to this first decree, Portuguese citizens were prohibited from capturing or buying Japanese nationals, and those Japanese who were already slaves must be freed; any Portuguese citizen who captured or bought Japanese nationals would have his entire wealth confiscated. The decree stipulates that one half of the confiscated wealth should become the property of the Kingdom of Portugal, and the other half would be granted to the person who prosecuted.[45]

The Jesuit Order in Japan issued a statement in 1596, saying that any Portuguese national who has engaged in slave trade should be excommunicated.[46] On April 16, 1597, the Viceroy in India issued the second decree in the name of the King of Portugal. According to this decree, any Japanese, regardless of his or her status, should not be forced to arrive at or reside in Macao.[47] However, there was no stipulation for punishment if anyone violated this decree. The Jesuit Order issued yet another statement in 1598, saying that engagement in slave trade shall result in excommunication and also in a fine of 10 cruzeiros per enslaved boy or girl.[48] It is not clear whether or not the same or similar stipulations were in the first statement. Around 1600, the King of Portugal issued a third decree, in which the validity of the first two decrees was confirmed.[49]

Looking at these actions from the common-sense perspective of the 21st century, one might assume that the King of Portugal and the Jesuit Order were motivated by humanitarian and ethical considerations. But that was definitely not the case. The motivation for these decrees and statements was completely different.

In reality there were two more practical reasons for their actions. First, many Portuguese in Asia were living corrupt lives, cohabiting with Japanese slave girls and totally ignoring the teaching of the Catholic Church. This problem had been pointed out repeatedly in documents written by the Portuguese themselves.[50] For example, when a ship from Macao sailing for India became stranded in 1583 in the Strait of Malacca, Diogo de Couto commented as follows: "Without fearing God, merchants and others keep fair-skinned and beautiful girls as concubines in the cabins of the ship. It is natural that God punishes such shameful acts. God makes them understand God's supreme power by the loss of a ship loaded with a large amount of cargo. Since the Portuguese in this region are engaging in immoral and lustful acts far more than in other regions of the world, there is no doubt that God threatened and punished them by causing typhoons many times."[51]

Gaspar Coelho thought that one of the reasons why Toyotomi Hideyoshi decided to prohibit Christianity was the immoral lives of Portuguese merchants. Coelho stated, "These merchants steal young, married women and make them their concubines. They kidnap children and bring them to their ships. Naturally, many of them commit suicide."[52] The immoral lives of the Portuguese were also mentioned in the Resolution of Excommunication issued by the Jesuit Order in 1598.[53]

Second, when the Portuguese bought slaves cheaply from Japan and the Korean Peninsula and then treated them as commodities, the reputation of the Christians as a whole was tarnished. This problem was clearly pointed out in a letter dated February 20, 1599 from the Jesuit Order in Japan to a provincial of the Jesuits in Portugal.[54] The purpose of the decrees and statements, then, was to prevent the Portuguese in Japan from degenerating further to the point of no return and also to improve the reputation of Christianity.

In brief, the Jesuit Order began to act against slavery because its own existence in Japan was threatened. The Jesuits in Japan knew quite well that the Portuguese were buying Japanese slaves and selling them overseas. Furthermore, they not only condoned Portuguese slave trade but also approved it officially. According to the Jesuits' second Proclamation of Excommunication from 1598 regarding those engaged in slave trade, the Jesuit Order in Japan kept approving the shipment of Japanese slave boys and girls by signing the document for shipment.[55] This clearly indicates that the Jesuits were officially approving the export of slaves.

The Effect of the Prohibition of Slavery

Despite the official decrees, statements, and laws on both the Japanese and the Portuguese sides, there was very little practical movement toward the termination of the slave trade. There are documents from as late as the 17th century in which Japanese slaves were shipped overseas.[56] The Portuguese nationals in Goa petitioned the King of Portugal in 1603 to end Japanese slavery. According to this document, there had been no improvement in terminating the slave trade after the first decree by the King of Portugal.[57] Attempts to follow the directives of the first decree were ignored and, for this reason, the decree was never honored. The Viceroy in India did not even appoint officers to carry out the decree.[58] The Portuguese colonies in India and other places in Asia simply ignored the new laws, and Portuguese merchants continued slave trade as if nothing had happened.

Japan also has two problems. First, feudal lords charged heavy taxes on peasants, and this forced many peasants to sell themselves or their family members into slavery. In response to Hideyoshi's harsh demand to terminate the slave trade, Gaspar Coelho replied that the most important thing was to prohibit feudal lords who were administering the harbors visited by foreign ships from allowing slave trade.[59]

Second, Japan was in a state of constant civil war when the Portuguese introduced firearms in 1543. Feudal lords immediately saw the superiority of guns over earlier weapons, and the Japanese soon began to produce firearms themselves in various places, such as Sakai, Kunitomo, Negoro, and Saiga, in response to their high demand.[60] However, the Japanese were unable to produce gunpowder. In order to produce it, the mineral niter was needed, but it did not exist naturally in Japan. Therefore, feudal lords were forced to rely on imported gunpowder in order to use firearms in battle. To them, having constant supplies of gunpowder meant a serious matter of survival. Some feudal lords went as far as getting baptized to get hold of gunpowder.[61]

In order to pay for the gunpowder they purchased, some feudal lords used slaves. King João III (John III) of Portugal's attributed remark confirms this: "Japan offers 50 slaves for a barrel of gunpowder." [62] The Jesuits called the coast along the Bay of Misumi in the Amakusa region of Kyushu "Silver Coast," because slaves were shipped from this area[63] and niter is silver in color.

Naturally, those who stood to lose from the prohibition of the slave trade were strongly against it. They were, for example, those Portuguese merchants in Goa who were actively involved in the slave trade. When they learned that the Jesuit Order in Japan excommunicated those involved in the slave trade in 1598, they sent two letters of protest to King Filipe II of Portugal in 1603 and 1605.

The first letter stated as follows: "Since the liberation of slaves would cause significant damage to the Portuguese living in India, we immediately met and discussed how to deal with this problem. We have spent one million cruzeiros or more over the years to purchase slaves. Furthermore, the Bishops and Fathers of the Jesuit Order who are in charge of Christianity in Japan have shown their acceptance of the purchase of slaves by issuing official documents of approval and permission. Therefore, we cannot accept that the King revokes this right and deprives us of the slaves we have already purchased." [64]

The letter also states, "Japanese are sold openly in Japan, and they are shipped to nearby Islamic countries and become Muslims. All of the Japanese bought by us become Christians, and this increases the subjects of the King of Portugal. Furthermore, after they have been educated by our Fathers for two years, they become free. If we Portuguese do not buy them as slaves, they become Muslims. In the Portuguese colony of India, there are many Japanese slaves. In an emergency, if a Portuguese national leads five or six Japanese slaves, each carrying a gun, that will be beneficial for us because the

Japanese are very warlike. When they are freed, they will not rebel against us by cooperating with our enemy countries. They are fewer than us in number, and there is no danger that they would kill us." [65]

The next letter from 1605 states as follows: "The first decree by the Portuguese King has never been carried out in reality during the past 30 years. The Portuguese Viceroy stationed in India never appointed officials to take care of this duty." [66] The letter also states: "Since slaves have been purchased on the basis of a goodwill contract, it is unjust to free slaves. A huge sum of money has been spent to purchase slaves, and if slaves are freed, some slave owners may lose as much as 1,000 to 2,000 cruzeiros. There are many who would end up in this situation." [67]

How did King Filipe II react? He issued yet another decree in March, 1605, stating as follows: "The earlier decrees had been applied broadly even to slaves legally owned with goodwill, and this affected the residents in India negatively. It has been reported that to free all Japanese slaves will result in significant financial damages. When there is a just and legal reason that is within the law, it is not my intention to prohibit the ownership of Japanese slaves. This was not the intention of the previous King Don Sebastian either. Since I received reports from the cities of Goa and Cochin, I have decided to issue a new decree for the sake of clarification. If a Japanese slave claims that he or she is held as a slave illegally, for an incorrect reason, examine the claim and try to free him or her in order to observe the law. Regarding this matter, I trust God and the judgment by those who serve me." [68]

In essence, King Filipe II is saying that if there is a legal and understandable explanation, slavery should be accepted. It was not his intention to free all slaves unconditionally, nor was this what

King Don Sebastian intended, according to his understanding.

The Reasons Why the Abolition of the Slave Trade Failed

Thus far, the following five points have been explained: First, the reasons Japanese were sold as slaves by the Portuguese; second, the conditions in Japanese society that enabled slavery; third, the reactions of the Portuguese kings and their representatives; fourth, the reactions of the Jesuits from Portugal stationed in Japan; and fifth, the reactions of the Portuguese in various Asian countries to the attempt to prohibit slavery. By reviewing these historical facts, we must conclude that attempts to ban slavery failed.

Every party involved in this problem reasoned and acted in terms of its own interests. Since there was a practice of selling people in Japan, due in part to the heavy taxes feudal lords charged on peasants, an undesirable but conceivable solution was to sell themselves into slavery. Here, the nationality of the broker or buyer becomes insignificant as long as peasants could solve their own problems. The feudal lords in Japan were involved in civil war, and in order to win, they needed firearms. Since they were forced to rely on imported gunpowder, some of them paid for it by offering slaves.

The Portuguese colonists needed an inexpensive labor force. They also wanted to have sexual relations of all kinds. For this reason, they needed both adults and children of both sexes. When there were supplies of slaves from Japan, the Portuguese bought them. Merchants engaged in slave trade when they realized they could make money from it.

Being Portuguese themselves, the Jesuits in Japan listened to what their fellow Portuguese in Japan were saying, and they were likely to support activities that were advantageous to the state of Portugal and to the Portuguese. In some cases, this led to the acceptance of slavery. At the same time, the key task of these Jesuits was to spread the Jesuit Order of Catholicism among the Japanese as much as possible. This meant they must avoid the danger of breeding hostile feelings among the Japanese against the Jesuit Order, the state of Portugal, and the Portuguese.

In order to deal with these conflicting issues, the Jesuits gave the impression that they were against slavery and, at the same time, condoned it. When Hideyoshi demanded harshly that the Portuguese must free Japanese slaves, the Jesuits felt the danger of becoming a Japanese enemy. They petitioned the Portuguese King to ban slavery and also enforced excommunication in order to appease Hideyoshi's fury. But despite what the decrees, rules, and resolutions said on paper, they were not enforced in reality. Everyone knew this. The slave trade continued as ever.

From the standpoint of the Portuguese kings, it was undesirable to be involved in international problems of this nature. The easiest way out for them was to make empty statements and let those directly involved handle the problem. Looking at the situation carefully, this is a familiar and universal problem of egoism---everyone thinks and acts according to his or her own benefits and safety. The victims in this particular situation were the Japanese men, women, boys and girls who, unfortunately, became slaves.

Japanese Actions

Already in 1587, Hideyoshi issued an order stating that, if a feudal lord desired to be converted to Christianity, he must obtain official permission from Hideyoshi himself. In reality, this meant that feudal lords were not allowed to become Christian. Hideyoshi confiscated the lands of Akashi because its lord, Takayama Ukon, defied this requirement and remained Christian.[69] Then, on July 25, 1587, Hideyoshi created a law expelling all missionaries from Japan.[70]

The so-called "San Felipe incident" of 1596 was a decisive event. A distressed Spanish ship named San Felipe sank near the island of Shikoku, but the accident had far-reaching results. According to the Japanese understanding of the incident, the Spanish crew on board proudly stated that Spain would first send missionaries to colonize the country and make the natives subservient, and, after that, Spain would send troops and occupy the country.[71] Since Hideyoshi was already very suspicious of these foreigners from Europe, he acted quickly. Foreign missionaries and converted Japanese were crucified in Nagasaki in 1596.

The details of this collective execution vary from one source to another. Catholics took this incident very seriously and depicted it in paintings but with a curious pattern: the Jesuits painted only three Jesuits, and the Franciscans painted only 23 Franciscans, excluding the three Jesuits. With only one exception, there were no paintings showing all who had been executed.[72] The Catholic Church recognized them as saints in 1862, and they were 26 in all.

Japanese sources vary as well. Tokutomi states there were six Franciscan missionaries and 20 converted Japanese,[73] while Onizuka states there were six Franciscans, three Jesuits, and 19 converted Japanese.[74] As Miyazaki suggests, the differences in the detail reflect the competition and conflict that existed among various Catholic orders in Japan, which included the Jesuits, the Franciscans, the Dominicans, and the Augustinians.[75]

Naturally, the relationship between Japan and Spain deteriorated. Tokugawa Ieyasu took over the position of head of state after Hideyoshi and became the first shogun of the Tokugawa family in 1603. He sent a diplomatic mission to Luzon (the Philippines), which was Spain's center of activity in east Asia. The Tokugawa government also sent a merchant from Kyoto named Tanaka Shosuke in 1610 on a diplomatic mission to Mexico, a Spanish colony, and tried to establish trade relations with the country. He was on board a Spanish ship that happened to have drifted to Chiba, near Edo (Tokyo). However, the mission was unsuccessful.

In 1612, the government resorted to drastic measures: Christianity was totally banned, Christian churches were demolished, and missionaries were expelled from the territories directly under the governmental administration. In 1613, the same policy was carried out across the entire nation in the form of the Christianity Prohibition Law.

After the enforcement of this law, the position of the Tokugawa government became harsher and harsher. In 1614, 300 Japanese, including Takayama Ukon, the feudal lord who refused to give up Christianity, were expelled from Japan to Luzon. In 1616, with the exception of Hirato and Nagasaki, all foreign ships except Chinese ones were forbidden to enter Japanese harbors. In 1624, Spaniards were no longer allowed to enter Japan. Around 1629, *fumie* began to be enforced. This was an unusual method of detecting Christians. According to this method, a suspected individual was required to step on a picture or a relief that showed some sort of Christian motif, such as a cross or the Madonna. If the suspected individual hesitated or refused, that was proof of being Christian, and he or she was to be prosecuted.

In 1636, the Portuguese in Japan were segregated from Japanese society and brought to Dejima, a small man-made island off the city of Nagasaki. In 1638, Christianity was absolutely forbidden. In 1639, Portuguese ships were totally forbidden to enter Japanese harbors. This meant that Portugal and Spain were completely expelled from Japan. Even British nationals who were not involved in the trade of Japanese slaves were excluded from Japan. The only Europeans not expelled were people from the Netherlands, but even in this case, they were required to stay on Dejima. In this way, Japan entered a period of total seclusion.

At the beginning of the age of colonialism, when European countries made contact with Japan, the policy of the Japanese authorities was to make a distinction between trade and missionary activity. Although Christianity was subsequently banned, trade was permitted. For example, even after the execution of missionaries and Japanese converts, Japan was trying to trade with Mexico, a Spanish colony. Japan also made a distinction between Catholic countries such as Portugal and Spain and non-Catholic countries such as the Netherlands and England. But these two groups of countries were known to slander each other.[76] This meant the Japanese were hearing negative and dangerous rumors about both sides. A logical solution for Japan, then, was to look at all these European countries suspiciously. In this sense, it is reasonable to think that, whether a country was Catholic or not, all Christian countries appeared suspicious and dangerous. The best solution for the Japanese was to choose the policy of seclusion.

An Interpretation of the Incidents

It is impossible to speculate about the consequences of a different chain of events in history. Speculation is speculation, nothing else. Therefore, it is impossible to imagine the direction of Japanese history if Hideyoshi acted differently and if Japan continued to maintain contact with these troublesome European countries. Nevertheless, one conceivable scenario is that Japan could have become a Catholic country, just like the Philippines and the colonies in Latin America. Another scenario is that Japan could have suffered from chronic and intense religious conflict. The hostility between Catholics and Protestants might have been reproduced in Japan.

When the Portuguese and the Spaniards began to establish contact with Japan, the most powerful feudal lord was Oda Nobunaga. He was receptive and looked favorably upon both the Portuguese and the Spaniards, including both missionaries and merchants, conceivably because he was interested in trade. Tachibana argues that Nobunaga was instrumental in spreading Christianity through hostile acts toward Buddhists.[77] When Luis Frois, a Portuguese national, sought permission to carry out missionary activities, Nobunaga granted it. Hideyoshi took control of the country after Nobunaga's death. Hideyoshi continued Nobunaga's policy toward the foreigners, but as soon as he learned about the slave trade by the Portuguese, he changed his view of the foreigners drastically.

From the standpoint of Hideyoshi, it was acceptable to sell and buy slaves in Japan, as slavery was a part of Japanese culture at the time. What he could not accept was foreigners exporting slaves from Japan without knowledge and without permission from him, the *de facto* head of the state. He understood that slaves were chained and treated like beasts. Christians were also demolishing Shinto shrines and Buddhist temples.

Even though it was true that Japanese slaves shipped overseas could become free after some years, they were in foreign countries, not in Japan. A freed slave in Japan could return to his or her native village, but when a freed slave was in a foreign country, it was far more difficult to return to Japan. These considerations were likely to underlie Hideyoshi's extremely hostile attitude toward the Portuguese involved in the slave trade.

Furthermore, the distance between various Portuguese leaders' words and their actions was enough to make the Japanese suspicious and hostile. It was natural to come to the conclusion that the country must take drastic action, and the San Felipe incident triggered just that. The execution of missionaries and converts, the total ban on Christianity, and the enforcement of a policy of seclusion can be easily and logically understandable from this perspective.

Conclusion

Japan's policy of seclusion became official in 1641. With minimal contact with the outside world, Japan was able to develop its own civilization in the form of, for example, *Genroku* culture. Commerce developed and incipient capitalism emerged. Japan was very much self-sufficient and basically peaceful under the Tokugawa shogunate. This was possible by not having troublesome Westerners in or around Japan.

Exactly for this reason, when the United States demanded that Japan must open up itself for diplomatic and commercial contact with the United States in 1853, the Japanese firmly rejected the demands. Because the Japanese rejection was firm and clear, the United States displayed its military and technological power fully, blackmailed, and threatened to occupy Japan.[78] When the Japanese came to terms with their military and technological inferiority, they were forced to yield to the American demand.

This was yet another infuriating experience in Japan's history. Abe Masahiro, who negotiated with the Americans as the chief representative of the Tokugawa shogunate, states that he "shed bloody tears." [79] Fukuzawa Yukichi, one of the leading thinkers of the time, wrote, "those in the Tokugawa government who carried out the task of opening Japan were all extreme xenophobes."[80]

This outrageous, traumatic, and painful experience with the Americans led to Japan's "modernization" and "Westernization" in order to fight back. The Japanese understood that in order to fight the West, Japan must have a Western military and Western technology.[81] This further led to Japan's own militarism and colonialism, to which the West responded with propaganda, policies, and political maneuvers that incited racism. The culmination of all these infuriating experiences resulted in the Pearl Harbor attack.[82] In this sense, it is possible to argue that Portuguese colonialism and slave trade resulted in totally unexpected consequences.[83]

Notes

1 There is some speculation that a Portuguese ship drifted to Usuki, Kyushu in 1541. See Onizuka, Hideaki, *Tenno no Rosario*, Ge. (Tokyo: Seiko Shobo, 2006), p.90.
2 Okamoto, Yoshitomo, *Jyuroku Seiki Nichio Kotsushi no Kenkyu*. (Tokyo: Hara Shobo, 1974), pp. 570, 728.
3 Yanagida, Toshio, "Umi o watatta Nihonjin Dorei," *Asahi Hyakka Sekai no Rekishi*, Vol. 69 (1990), p. D-438.
4 Gunji, Kiichi, *Jyunana Seiki ni okeru Nissen Kankei*. (Tokyo: Gaimusho Chosabu, 1934), p. 534.
5 Satow, Ernest, "Note on the Intercourse between Japan and Siam in the Seventeenth Century," *Transactions of the Asiatic Society of Japan*, Vol. 13, 1885, p.182.
6 Gunji, *op. cit.*, p. 534.
7 Guerreiro, Fernão, *Relação Anual das Coisas que Fizeram os Padres da Companhia de Jesus*, II. (Coimbra: Impr. Da Universidade,1930), p.312.
8 *Ibid.*, p. 312.
9 Gunji, *op. cit.*, p. 537.
10 Okamoto, *op. cit.*, p. 778.
11 Yanagida, *op. cit.*, p. D-438.
12 Ohtsuka, Makoto, "Raten Amerika ni okeru Nihonjin Jiyu Tokomin no Tenmatsu," *Mita Hyoron*, March (2000), pp.72-5.
13 Inoue, Mitsuo, et al, *Rikai Shiyasui Nihonshi B*. (Tokyo: Buneido, 1995), p. 163.
14 *Ibid.*, p. 163.
15 *De Missione Legatorum Iaponen Anno 1590*, translated into Japanese by Izumi Kyunosuke et al as *De Sande Tensho Ken'o Shisetsu Ki*. (Tokyo:Yushodo Shoten, 1969), p. 233.
16 Ohtsuka, *op. cit.*, p. 73.
17 *Goryeo Sa Choryo*, Vol. 28, (1452).
18 Inoue, et al, *op. cit.*, p. 132.
19 Akiyama, Kenzo, "Wako ni yoru Chosen-Shinajin Dorei no Ryakudatsu to

sono Sokan oyobi Baibai," *Shakai Keizai Shi Gakkai*, Vol. 2, No. 8 (1932), pp.811-839.

20 Okamoto, *op. cit.*, p. 766.

21 *Ibid.*, P. 730.

22 Barros, João de, *Da Asia, Nova Edição* (originally Lisboa,1778; Coimbra: Impr. Da Universidade, 1932), Dec. III, Liv., Cap. II.

23 Pagés, Leon, *Histoire de la religion chrétienne au Japon depuis 1598 jusqu'a 1651*, II.(Paris:C. Douniol,1869-70), p. 72, 73.

24 Frois, Luis, *Apparatos para a Historia Ecclestiastica do Bispado de Japão* (Lisboa, 1812), fl. 267v.

25 Okamoto, *op. cit.*, p. 763.

26 Storck, Wilhelm, *Vida e Obras de Luis Camões.* (Lisboa: Academia Real das Sciencias, 1898), pp. 586, 652.

27 Okamoto, *op. cit.*, pp. 757-764.

28 Pagés, *op. cit.*, II, pp. 72-74.

29 *Ibid.*, pp. 73, 74.

30 *Ibid.*, pp. 74, 75; Frois, *op. cit.*, I, fl. 495; *op. cit.*, II, fls. 23v, 24.

31 Pagés, *op.cit.*, II, pp. 74, 75.

32 *Ibid.*, pp. 74, 75.

33 Avila Girón, Bernardino, "Relación del Reino del Nippon," *Archivo Ibero-Americano*, Año XXI, No.113, p.34; Frois, *op. cit.*, II, fls. 23v, 24; *op. cit.*,I, fl. 495.

34 Tachibana, Kyoko, *Nobunaga to Jyujika.* (Tokyo: Shuei Sha, 2004).

35 *Kyushu Godoza Ki* (1587). The full document is reproduced in Shimizu Hirokazu, *Shoku-ho Seiken to Kirishitan.* (Tokyo: Iwata Shoten, 2001), p.405.

36 Tokutomi Iichiro, *Kinsei Nihon Kokumin Shi, Toyotomi Jidai, Otsu.* (Tokyo: Minyu Sha, 1920), pp. 379-80.

37 *Cartas qve os Padres e Irmãos de Companhia de Iesus escreuerão dos Reynos de Iapão & China aos da mesma Companhia da India, & Europa, desdo anno de 1549, até o de 1580.* (Evora, 1598), II, fl. 108.

38 Frois, *op. cit.*, I.; Frois, Luis, *Historia do Japão*, edição anotada por Jose Wicki. (Lisboa: Biblioteca Nacional, 1776)

39 *Ibid.*, fl. 481.

40 Pagés, *op. cit.*, pp. 73, 76.

41 Okamoto, *op. cit.*, p. 740.

42 *Ibid.*, p. 740.

43 *Ibid.*, p. 741.
44 Yanagida, Toshio, "Toyotomi Hideyoshi Indo Fukuo ate Shokan Anbun ni tsuite," *Biburia*, No. 88, May, 1987, pp.55, 59.
45 de J. H. Da Cunha Rivara, Ed., *Archivo Portuguez-Oriental.* (Nova-Goa, 1857-1875), Fusc. V, Pt. II, pp. 791, 792.
46 No document remains but this is referred to in the document from 1598.
47 de J. H. Da Cunha Rivara, *op. cit.*, Fusc. III, pp. 763, 764.
48 Pagés, *op. cit.*, p. 71.
49 de J. H. Da Cunha Rivara, *op. cit.*, Fusc. I, Pt. II, p. 125.
50 Ayres, Christovao, *Fernao Mendes Pinto.* (Lisboa, 1905), p.89.
51 Couto, Diogo de, *Da Asia.* (originally 1602-1645; Lisboa: Na Regia Officina Typografica, 1777-1788), dec. X, liv. III, Cap. XIV.
52 Delplace, Louis, *S. Francois-Xavier et ses premiers successeurs, 1540-43 (Le Catholicisme au Japon,* I), (Bruxelles: Libr. Albert Dewit, 1909).
53 Pagés, *op. cit.*, II, p. 76.
54 Izawa, Minoru, "Tsusho Hiwa:Nihonjin Yushutsu Ko," *Tokyo Asahi Shimbun,* July 11, 1932.
55 Pagés, *op. cit.*, II, p. 71.
56 Tokutomi, *op. cit.*, p. 748.
57 de J. H. Cunha Rivara, *op. cit.*, Fasc. I, Pt. II, p. 125.
58 *Ibid.*, Fasc. I, Pt. II, pp. 125, 127.
59 Frois, *op. cit.*, I, fl. 481.
60 Inoue, et al., *op. cit.*, p. 160.
61 Onizuka, *op. cit.*, p. 107, 110.
62 *Ibid.*, p. 117.
63 *Ibid.*, p. 106, 107, 110.
64 de J. H. da Cunha Rivara, *op. cit.*, Fasc. I, Pt. II, pp. 125, 126.
65 *Ibid.*, Fasc. I, Pt. II, p. 127.
66 *Ibid.*, Fasc. I, Pt. II, p. 157.
67 *Ibid.*, Fasc. I, Pt. II, p. 157.
68 *Documentos Remetidos da India ou Livros das Monções.* (Lisboa:Publicação da Academia Real das Sciencias de Lisboa, 1883-1893), p. 43; Takase, Koichiro, ed. and tr., *Monsun Bunsho to Nihon: Jyunana Seiki Porutogaru Kobunsho Shu,* (Tokyo: Yagi Shoten, 2006), pp. 131-132.
69 Inoue, et al., *op. cit.*, p. 168.
70 Tokutomi, *op. cit.*, pp. 388-389.

71 Tokutomi, *op. cit.*, p. 21; Inoue, et al., *op. cit.*, p. 168. But this widely held understanding is questioned by Matsuda. See Matsuda, Kiichi, *Hideyoshi no Nanban Gaiko.* (Tokyo: Shin Jinbutsu Orai Sha, 1972), p. 278.

72 Miyazaki, Kentaro, "Kirishitan Jidai ni okeru Iezusu Kai Nihon Kanku no Jinteki Kousei to Hyouka ni tsuite", in Yanai Kenji, Ed., *Sakoku Nihon to Kokusai Koryu,* Jyoukan. (Tokyo: Yoshikawa Kobun Kan, 1988), p. 81.

73 Tokutomi, *op. cit.*, p. 22.

74 Onizuka, *op. cit.*, p. 102.

75 Miyazaki, *op. cit.*, pp. 80, 81.

76 Inoue, *op. cit.*, p. 191.

77 Tachibana, *op. cit.*, p. 175.

78 Kitahara, Michio, *Children of the Sun.* (New York: St. Martin's Press, 1989), Chapters 2, 3.

79 Nakane, Sekko, *Sakumu Kiji,* Vol. 1. (Tokyo: Nihon Shiseki Kyokai, 1920; originally 1853-1858), p. 159.

80 Fukuzawa Yukichi, "Fukuo Jiden," in Keio Gijyuku, Ed., *Fukuzawa Yukichi Zenshu,* Vol. 7. (Tokyo: Iwanami Shoten, 1959; originally 1899), pp. 147-8.

81 Kitahara, Michio, "The Rise of Four Mottoes in Japan," *Journal of Asian History,* Vol. 20, No. 1, 1986, pp. 54-57; Kitahara, Michio, *op. cit.*, Chapters 4, 5, 6.

82 Kitahara, Michio, *Naze Taiheiyo Senso ni nattanoka.* (Tokyo: TBS-Britannica, 2001).

83 The economists and philosophers of the so-called "Austrian School" emphasize the unexpected consequences of human behavior as one of the key assumptions of their research. See, for example, Menger, Carl, *Investigations into the Method of the Social Sciences with Special Reference to Economics,* (New York: New York University Press, 1985), pp. 139-59; and Mises, Ludwig von, *Human Action.* (Chicago: Henry Regnery, 1966), pp. 92-118.

北原　惇（きたはら じゅん）

本名は北原順男（きたはら みちお）。
1937年生まれ。横浜出身。武蔵高校卒。1961年モンタナ大学（米国モンタナ州ミゾーラ市）卒（社会学と人類学の二専攻）。1968年ウプサラ大学（スウェーデン）修士課程修了（社会学専攻）。1971年ウプサラ大学博士課程修了（社会心理学専攻）。同年哲学博士号を受ける。メリーランド大学、ミシガン大学、サンフランシスコ大学、ニューヨーク州立大学（バッファロ）などでの教職、研究職を経て1997年までノーデンフェルト・インスティテュート（スウェーデン・イエテボリ市）所長。
マーキーズ・フーズフーその他海外約20のフーズフーに経歴収載。英語の著書は *Children of the Sun* (Macmillan, 1989)、*The Tragedy of Evolution* (Praeger, 1991)、*The Entangled Civilization* (University Press of America, 1995)、*The African Revenge* (Phoenix Archives, 2003) など。日本語の著書は『なぜ太平洋戦争になったのか』(TBSブリタニカ、2001)、『幼児化する日本人』（リベルタ出版、2005年）、『生き馬の目を抜く西洋文明』（実践社、2006年）、『ロック文化が西洋を滅ぼす』（花伝社、2007年）、『黄色に描かれる西洋人』（花伝社、2007年）、『現代音楽と現代美術にいたる歴史』（花伝社、2009年）、『脱西洋の民主主義へ』（花伝社、2009年）。

ポルトガルの植民地形成と日本人奴隷

2013年2月25日　初版第1刷発行

著者　──北原　惇
発行者　──平田　勝
発行　──花伝社
発売　──共栄書房
〒101-0065　東京都千代田区西神田2-5-11出版輸送ビル2F
電話　　03-3263-3813
FAX　　03-3239-8272
E-mail　kadensha@muf.biglobe.ne.jp
URL　　http://kadensha.net
振替　　00140-6-59661
装幀　──佐々木正見
印刷・製本──シナノ印刷株式会社

ⓒ2013　北原惇
ISBN978-4-7634-0657-6 C0020

花伝社　北原惇の本

ロック文化が西洋を滅ぼす
――脳科学から見た文明論

定価（本体 1600 円＋税）

●西洋はなぜ滅びるのか？
いじめ、落書き、暴力犯罪、騒音公害、麻薬、性の乱脈、礼儀知らずなどがなぜ日本でもあたりまえになってしまったのか……。西洋の社会問題は西洋の文化圏に組み込まれてしまった日本の社会問題である。ユニークな「脳科学の知見にもとづく文明論」。
◆推薦　二木宏明　東大名誉教授（心理学者・脳科学者）◆
著者の問題意識がひしひしと伝わってくる。読ませる本である。一読をお薦めする。

黄色に描かれる西洋人
――思想史としての西洋の人種主義

定価（本体 1600 円＋税）

●破綻する「白人」思想
人種主義から考察する現代文明論。自らを「白人」と呼ぶ西洋の人種主義は侵略と植民地化を正当化するエゴイズム。人種をドグマ的に色で表現する西洋の人種主義に変化が現れ始めた。だが西洋という強者と同一視する心理によって西洋文明を受け入れてしまった日本では、西洋の人種主義を何の疑問もなく信じている。「新しい歴史教科書」にもそのことが端的に現れている……。

現代音楽と現代美術にいたる歴史
――動物学と脳科学から見た芸術論

定価（本体 2000 円＋税）

●脳科学と動物学の成果にもとづいて、今日にいたる芸術の歴史をつらぬく原理を解明
終始不可解な音の連続で美しさも楽しさも感じられない音楽、何を表現しているのか理解できない絵画、ゴミとしか見えない作品……。
なぜ現代芸術は美的体験からほど遠くなってしまったのか？
◆推薦　二木宏明　東大名誉教授（心理学者・脳科学者）◆
動物行動学と脳科学の知見を踏まえたユニークな切り口からの芸術論。前著、『ロック文化が西洋を滅ぼす』同様、読ませる本である。

脱西洋の民主主義へ
――多様性・負の自由・直接民主主義

定価（本体 2000 円＋税）

●ほとんど違いのない二大政党による政治は、二党独裁と呼ぶべきである
生物的・心理的・文化的に多様な世界の人びと。西洋文明から世界に広められた「民主主義」は、人間の多様性を十分に考慮しているだろうか？　個人個人の尊厳を最優先にするためには、過半数による多数決・政党制を軸とする今日の「民主主義」のままでよいのだろうか？